SEVEN DAYS AND SALVATION

Loretta VandenBrink

WESTBOW
P R E S S®
A DIVISION OF THOMAS NELSON
& ZONDERVAN

All Scripture quotes and references are taken from the King James Version of the Bible, copyright 2017 Published by Thomas Nelson.

This book is a work of non-fiction. Unless otherwise noted, the author and the publisher make no explicit guarantees as to the accuracy of the information contained in this book and in some cases, names of people and places have been altered to protect their privacy.

WestBow Press books may be ordered through booksellers or by contacting:

WestBow Press
A Division of Thomas Nelson & Zondervan
1663 Liberty Drive
Bloomington, IN 47403
www.westbowpress.com
1 (866) 928-1240

ISBN: 978-1-9736-5514-5 (sc)
ISBN: 978-1-9736-5513-8 (hc)
ISBN: 978-1-9736-5515-2 (e)

Library of Congress Control Number: 2019902373

Print information available on the last page.

WestBow Press rev. date: 03/27/2019

DEDICATION

This book is dedicated to Denny, my husband of forty-six years; our sons, Craig and John; Wendy, Craig's wife of twenty-two years; and their three children, Jessica, Nicole, and Wyatt.

This book is also dedicated to my aunt Esther, to whom I am grateful for her continual encouragement and prayers.

ACKNOWLEDGEMENT

I would like to thank Kathy Ide, co-owner of the Christian Editor Network, for her work in editing this book. I could not have done this without the expertise of a professional like her ... Kathy truly was God's answer to my prayer.

CONTENTS

Chapter 1 Show Me Your Glory.. 1

Chapter 2 The Counsel of the Lord 13

Chapter 3 Day 2 – The Firmament.. 25

Chapter 4 Day 3 – Brought Forth...33

Chapter 5 Day 4 – Two Great Lights 47

Chapter 6 Day 5 – Ancient Of Days 59

Chapter 7 Day 6 – The Blood..69

Chapter 8 Day 7 – The Generations Of Men.......................79

Chapter 9 To Day 91

INTRODUCTION

Many believe the first chapter of Genesis is the story of creation, but God did not express His eternal power and divine nature for the sake of creation. He expressed Himself in His power to save mankind from sin.

Moses, John, and Paul all agree, salvation can be seen not in what God created (something new), but in the things God made (fashioned).

Moses wrote God made (not created) the firmament (Genesis 1:7), the two great lights (Genesis 1:16), and the beast of the earth (Genesis 1:25).

John wrote "In the beginning was the Word, and the Word was with God, and the Word was God. The same was in the beginning with God. All things were **made** by him; and without him was not any thing **made** that was **made**." (John 1:1–3)

The Apostle Paul wrote "For the invisible things of him from the creation of the world are clearly seen, being understood by the things that are **made**, even his eternal power and Godhead;" (Romans 1:20).

In this book we will read about Job, Stephen, the Samaritan woman who talked with Jesus at the well outside the city of Sychar, John, Peter, and Paul. They will guide us through the orderly fashion in which God brought life to the Earth and made a way for mankind to be saved from sin … before God created man.

CHAPTER 1

SHOW ME YOUR GLORY

Traditionally we have been taught that the first chapter of Genesis is the story of creation and that each of the six days ended with God saying it was good. But has tradition steered us wrong? We are about to find out as we probe into the writings of Moses for each day. Then by comparing his writings to the other books of the Bible, we will determine whether Moses was writing about creation or ... was he writing about God's power for salvation.

Moses was a faithful servant of God. He testified to things that God said would take place in the future (Hebrews 3:5). God did not speak to him in visions or dreams, or with questions or parables. He spoke with Moses clearly and directly, "mouth to mouth" (Numbers 12:6–8), as if taking in a breath of air. Jesus said "For had ye believed Moses, ye would have believed me: for he wrote of me." (John 5:46).

Moses was eighty years old when God spoke to him from the burning bush. It was his obedience to God that brought him to the place of seeing God's glory; this is Moses' story.

Moses was a descendant of Abraham, Isaac, and Jacob. He was born in Egypt during a time when Pharaoh wanted all male Hebrew babies killed. As a newborn, Moses was kept hidden by his mother for three months. When she could no longer hide him, she placed him into a woven basket and laid it in the reeds along the bank of the Nile River. Moses was rescued by Pharaoh's daughter, who raised him as her own son (Exodus 1:15–2:10).

When Moses was forty years old he killed an Egyptian while defending an Israelite (Acts 7:23–24). Knowing Pharaoh wanted him dead, Moses left Egypt and went to Midian (Exodus 2:15).

Moses was on Mount Horeb (also known as Mount Sinai) in Midian, tending a flock belonging to his father-in-law Jethro, when God spoke to him from a burning bush. He asked Moses to go to Egypt and tell Pharaoh to let the Israelites leave Egypt. God promised Moses, "Certainly I will be with thee; and this shall be a token unto thee, that I have sent thee: When thou hast brought forth the people out of Egypt, ye shall serve God upon this mountain." (Exodus 3:12).

THE LOCATION OF MOUNT SINAI

The maps found in the back of many Bibles place Midian east of the Sinai Peninsula. Those same maps show Mount Sinai in the southern portion of the Sinai Peninsula, but fail to show the

Mount Sinai in Midian. The apostle Paul said the biblical Mount Sinai is in the land of Arabia (Galatians 4:25).

Helena, the mother of the Roman Emperor Constantine, named the mount in the southern portion of the Sinai Peninsula "Mount Sinai". Saint Catherine's Monastery is located there. There is no evidence to support this location as the biblical Mount Sinai.

It would have been impossible for the Israelites to cross through the Red Sea (as the Bible says they did) if the biblical Mount Sinai was located in the southern tip of the Sinai Peninsula. (For more information watch the documentary *The Search for the Real Mt. Sinai,* with John Rhys Davies, Larry Williams, and Bob Cornuke.)

MOSES IN EGYPT

Moses was eighty years old when he and his brother Aaron first spoke to Pharaoh (Exodus 7:7). Pharaoh not only refused to let God's people go, he demanded they work harder. This caused the Israelites to become angry with Moses (Exodus 5:6–21). God then gave four promises to Moses for the children of Israel.

> Wherefore say unto the children of Israel, I am the Lord, and **I will bring you out** from under the burdens of the Egyptians, and **I will rid you out of their bondage**, and **I will redeem you** with a stretched out arm, and with great judgments: and **I will take you to me** for a people, and I will be to you a God: and ye shall know that I am the Lord

your God, which bringeth you out from under the burdens of the Egyptians. (Exodus 6:6–7)

God sent nine plagues to ravage the land. The night of the tenth plague a lamb was roasted for each family to eat, and possibly for a neighbor as well, since there were to be no leftovers. Everyone ate with coats on and walking sticks in hand, ready to leave in a hurry.

At midnight an eerie silence filled the air, not even a dog barked. The invisible presence of darkness settled in. The Israelites sighed a breath of relief when death passed over their houses, and they were thankful for the blood that covered their doorposts.

A shout was heard. "Hurry! It is time to go!" Hundreds of thousands of Israelites left their homes, knowing they would never return.

As they hurried to leave Rameses, the sound of loud wailing filled the air. Every firstborn of the Egyptians had died, both people and beasts, because their houses were not marked with the blood of a lamb.

Three days later the Israelites passed through the Red Sea on dry ground while Pharaoh and his entire army drowned in the sea.

Three months later Moses and the Israelites were in Midian at the base of Mount Sinai (Exodus 19:1–2).

While the Israelites camped there, Moses climbed Mount Sinai to meet with God. The Lord sent him back down the mount to ask the Israelites if they would obey Him (Exodus 19:3–6).

The next time Moses climbed Mount Sinai was to give the Lord the people's answer: yes, they would do all that He had said (Exodus 19:8). God sent Moses back down to sanctify the people and to place boundaries at the base of the mountain. In three days He would descend on Mount Sinai to talk to the people (Exodus 19:10–15).

"And it came to pass on the third day in the morning, that there were thunders and lightnings, and a thick cloud upon the mount, and the voice of the trumpet exceedingly loud; so that all the people that was in the camp trembled." (Exodus 19:16). Moses brought the people out of the camp to meet with God. Moses spoke and God answered him in an audible voice (Exodus 19:17–19).

"The Lord came down upon mount Sinai, on the top of the mount: and the Lord called Moses up to the top of the mount; and Moses went up." (Exodus 19:20). This was the third time since coming out of Egypt that Moses climbed Mount Sinai to meet with God. God instructed Moses to go back down and warn the people they must not cross the boundaries at the bottom of the mountain or they would perish (Exodus 19:21–25).

Moses was with the people at the base of Mount Sinai when God first spoke His commandments (Exodus 20:1–17). The Israelites heard God's voice only as the noise of a very loud trumpet. Fearing they would die, the Israelites stood far away from the mount and asked Moses to tell them what God said. From then on God never spoke directly to the Israelites; He spoke only to Israel's spiritual leaders.

The fourth time Moses climbed Mount Sinai he drew even nearer to God. He was given the laws and rules the people were to live by. Moses returned to the people and told them all the Lord had said. Answering with one voice they agreed to do everything the Lord said. Moses wrote down all the words of the Lord, built an altar, and set up twelve pillars. Animals were sacrificed for the atonement of the sins of the people, and Moses read the book of the covenant to the people. As a seal of the blood covenant the sacrificial blood was sprinkled upon the altar and on the people (Exodus 20:21–24:8).

Aaron and his sons Nadab and Abihu, along with seventy elders, were with Moses as he climbed Mount Sinai for the fifth time. Only Moses could approach the Lord; the others were to worship at a distance.

The sixth time Moses climbed Mount Sinai, God gave him the tablets of stone on which He had written His law and commandments (Exodus 24:12–13). God became angry and asked Moses to leave so He could destroy the Israelites (Abraham's descendants) and make Moses and his descendants into a great nation (Exodus 32:9–10).

Four hundred and thirty years earlier God gave the land of Canaan (now Israel) to Abraham and his descendants as their inheritance (Genesis 15:18; Exodus 12:40–41). That covenant was sealed with God's word (Hebrews 6:13), and would never change (Numbers 23:19; Malachi 3:6; James 1:17).

Moses validated his trust in God saying, "Remember Abraham, Isaac, and Israel, thy servants, to whom thou swarest by thine own self, and saidst unto them, I will multiply your seed as the stars of heaven, and all this land that I have spoken of will I give unto your seed, and **they shall inherit it for ever**." (Exodus 32:13).

Moses made his way down Mount Sinai and along the way he encountered Joshua, who was waiting for him. Sensing there was trouble, Joshua warned Moses of the sounds he'd heard coming from the Israelite camp. He described them as the sounds of war. But Moses disagreed, saying the noise he heard was like singing (Exodus 32:17–18).

Moses was right. The Israelites were singing—to a golden calf, claiming it to be their god!

Burning with anger, Moses threw down the stone tablets at the base of Mount Sinai where they broke into pieces (Exodus 32.19). He burned the golden calf, crushed and ground it until it was as fine as dust, and threw it into the brook that flowed down Mount Sinai (Deuteronomy 9:21).

God then told Moses that because the people were so stiff-necked they would be destroyed if God went with them. Therefore, an angel would accompany them. This caused the people to mourn (Exodus 33:1–6).

Moses took the tent of meeting far outside the camp and called it the tabernacle of the congregation. God met with Moses there, talking with him face-to-face as a man would speak to a friend (Exodus 33:7–11). This is their conversation, as quoted from Exodus.

> Moses: Now therefore, I pray thee, if I have found grace in thy sight, shew me now thy way, that I may know thee, that I may find grace in thy sight: and consider that this nation is thy people.

> God: My presence shall go with thee, and I will give thee rest.

Moses: If thy presence go not with me, carry us not up hence. For wherein shall it be known here that I and thy people have found grace in thy sight? is it not in that thou goest with us? so shall we be separated, I and thy people, from all the people that are upon the face of the earth.

God: I will do this thing also that thou hast spoken: for thou hast found grace in my sight, and I know thee by name.

Moses: **I beseech thee, shew me thy glory**.

God: I will make all my goodness pass before thee, and I will proclaim the name of the Lord before thee; and will be gracious to whom I will be gracious, and will shew mercy on whom I will shew mercy.

God: Thou canst not see my face: for there shall no man see me, and live.

God: Behold, there is a place by me, and thou shalt stand upon a rock: and it shall come to pass, while my glory passeth by, that I will put thee in a clift of the rock, and will cover thee with my hand while I pass by: and I will take away mine hand, and thou shalt see my back parts: but my face shall not be seen.

(Exodus 33:13–23)

Realizing that he was about to see God's glory, Moses probably didn't get much sleep the night before he climbed Mount Sinai for the seventh time. Surely there was an excitement in his heart like he had never felt before as he arose early the next morning.

The Lord stood Moses in the cleft of a rock and placed His hand in front of Moses's face. As the Lord passed before him Moses heard the Lord proclaim:

> The Lord, the Lord God, merciful and gracious, longsuffering, and abundant in goodness and truth, Keeping mercy for thousands, forgiving iniquity and transgression and sin, and that will by no means clear the guilty; visiting the iniquity of the fathers upon the children, and upon the children's children, unto the third and to the fourth generation. (Exodus 34:6–7)

When God removed His hand from the face of Moses, seeing only God's backside, he saw into eternity past. Knowing God had created the heaven and the earth, Moses saw the six days God established salvation on the earth, and the seventh day when He rested from all His work. Moses described those days as "the generations of the heavens and of the earth when they were created, in the day that the Lord God made the earth and the heavens." (Genesis 2:4).

Moses was on Mount Sinai for forty days and forty nights

before he came down with the second set of stone tablets, on which was inscribed the "words of the covenant, the ten commandments" (Exodus 34:28). God's work for salvation would be made known in the tabernacle, the law, and God's feast days. They are the shadows in the Old Testament to Jesus Christ in the New Testament.

The first thing Aaron and the Israelites noticed about Moses when he came down from Mount Sinai this time was that his face was radiant—so much so that they were afraid to go near him (Exodus 34:30).

Moses obeyed God and built the ark of the covenant, the tabernacle, and all its furnishings, down to the finest of details, including the color of the threads that were woven together for the veil that hung before the Holy of Holies. He taught the people God's laws, and they celebrated God's feast days, which we now know represent Jesus' crucifixion, death, and resurrection, God sending His Holy Spirit, and the second coming of Jesus Christ.

On the first day of the first month of the second year after coming out of Egypt, Moses set up the tabernacle. When he did, the glory of the Lord filled it. (Exodus 40:17–35).

Forty years after going to Egypt, at the age of 120, Moses died. Until the day of his death, his eyes were not weak, nor was his physical strength gone (Deuteronomy 34:7). Moses was the meekest man to have ever lived (Numbers 12:3), and no other prophet in Israel spoke face-to-face with God as Moses did (Deuteronomy 34:10).

This brings us to the first chapter of Genesis. Moses, having seen the glory of God, was writing about salvation. In the beginning God created the heaven and the earth, and Moses,

God's faithful servant, from the beginning testified to things that would be spoken of in the future (Hebrews 3:5), he wrote about Jesus (John 5:46).

GOD IS THE CREATOR

Hast thou not known? hast thou not heard, that the everlasting God, the Lord, the Creator of the ends of the earth, fainteth not, neither is weary? there is no searching of his understanding. (Isaiah 40:28)

GOD IS THE MAKER

Thus saith the Lord, the Holy One of Israel, and his Maker, Ask me of things to come concerning my sons, and concerning the work of my hands command ye me. I have made the earth, and created man upon it: I, even my hands, have stretched out the heavens, and all their host have I commanded. (Isaiah 45:11–12)

GOD IS I AM

God said unto Moses, I AM THAT I AM: and he said, Thus shalt thou say unto the children of Israel, I AM hath sent me unto you. (Exodus 3:14)

CHAPTER 2

THE COUNSEL OF THE LORD

Moses heard the Lord proclaiming Himself the God of salvation … a merciful and gracious God, longsuffering, abundant in goodness and truth (Exodus 34:6). Then seeing into eternity past he saw:

> The earth was without form, and void; and darkness
> was upon the face of the deep. (Genesis 1:2).

Moses doesn't say how the earth came to be without form and void, but surely it is not how God created it. Nor does Moses explain the darkness or where the face of the deep is.

Lucifer is one of three archangels named in the Bible. Pride and jealousy changed this angel into darkness, and his name to Satan, which means "adversary" (of God). The prophets Isaiah and Ezekiel spoke of Satan being thrown to the ground (Isaiah 14:12–14; Ezekiel 28:12–19). Jesus said he saw Satan as lighting fall from heaven (Luke 10:18). Was Satan the darkness that was upon the face of the deep? Did Satan's fall from heaven cause the earth to be without form and void?

God did create many types of angels (Job 38:7). He placed cherubim with flaming swords to guard the way of the tree of life (Genesis 3:24). Isaiah writes of seraphim (Isaiah 6:2), Daniel of archangels (Daniel 10:13), and Matthew of guardian angels (Matthew 18:10). The angel Gabriel is a messenger of God (Luke 1:19). All angels were created by God to minister to the heirs of salvation (Hebrews 1:14). Some of the angles did fall away from God, but there is an innumerable company of angels (Hebrews 12:22) at work to defend and protect believers in Jesus Christ from all harm (Psalm 91:9–16).

God would make it known that He restored the earth from when it was formless and void. By His Divine power He gave life to the earth. God revealed this by teaching Job that his good works didn't have the power to save him from sin.

Job was a wealthy and devout man of God who lived in the land of Uz, a territory linked to Edom, which is believed to have been located southeast of the Dead Sea.

When Satan, the ruler of the darkness (Ephesians 6:12), came before God with the angels of God, God asked him where he had come from. Satan said he had been going to and fro in the earth, walking up and down in it (Job 1:6–7).

Jesus warned us about Satan, saying, "The thief cometh not, but for to steal, and to kill, and to destroy: I am come that they might have life, and that they might have it more abundantly" (John 10:10). And Peter cautions us to be sober and vigilant because our adversary, the devil, like a roaring lion, walks about the earth, seeking whom he may devour (1 Peter 5:8).

God, knowing that Satan had failed in his attempts to devour Job, asked him, "Hast thou considered my servant Job, that there is none like him in the earth, a perfect and an upright man, one that feareth God, and escheweth evil?" (Job 1:8).

Satan, who is a liar and the father of liars (John 8:44), defended himself by accusing Job of only seeming to be upright and perfect. He insisted that if God were to remove His hand of protection, Job would curse God (Job 1:9–11).

We know that Satan is allowed to test our faith. James wrote that we are to count it all joy when our faith is tested (James 1:2–4). Paul said that faith comes by hearing the word of God (Romans 10:17), and when putting on the whole armor of God faith is our shield of protection (Ephesians 6:10–18).

Job's reverence toward God and his good works was not a substitute for faith in God, and didn't keep what Job feared most from happening to him (Job 3:25). Job endured tremendous personal loss when Satan came at him. Within one day all of Job's children were killed and all of his wealth was gone. Although Satan had stolen everything from him, Job did not curse God (Job 1:13–22).

Satan came before God a second time, claiming that Job didn't curse God because he still had his health. So God allowed Satan to affect Job's health but not to kill him.

Satan struck Job with sores from the soles of his feet to the top of his head. Job's condition was so horrific that when his friends saw him they didn't recognize him and they wept (Job 2:1–13).

For seven days Job's three friends sat with him without saying a word. Finally Job spoke. He said he believed his losses were a punishment for sin. Yet he hadn't sinned; he was in right standing with God.

His friends insisted that God would not punish him if he hadn't sinned. They debated this for twenty-nine chapters. In the end Job's friends stopped answering Job "because he was righteous in his own eyes" (Job 32:1).

A young man named Elihu, who because of his youth had been holding back from saying anything, finally spoke up. Elihu was angry with Job for justifying himself, and he was angry with Job's friends because they could not disprove Job (Job 32:2–3). Elihu tried to persuade Job that his righteousness did not have the power to keep him from disaster.

After six chapters of this, the Lord Jehovah, the living and eternal God, made a powerful entrance into their conversation, questioning Job:

> Who is this that darkeneth **counsel** by words without knowledge? (Job 38:2)

Job, believing his works should have saved him, was then warned by God that he'd better brace himself. God is going to question him, and He demanded Job answer. Satan's next attack would kill him, and whether Job lived or died depended upon his answer … would he agree with God.

Gird up now thy loins like a man; for I will demand of thee, and answer thou me. Where wast thou when **I laid the foundations of the earth?** declare, if thou hast understanding. (Job 38:3–4)

Using the Jewish method of teaching, which is to teach by asking questions, God asked Job "Where were you?" If your good works have the power to save you from sickness and death, then where you when I (God the Father, Son, and Holy Spirit) laid the foundations of the earth? I fixed and established the earth restoring it to life from when it was formless and void. Tell Me, do you have the power to restore life?

God's next question was:

Who hath laid the measures thereof, if thou knowest? or who hath stretched the line upon it? (Job 38:5)

Now God is not questioning Job about the power it took to restore the earth. God is questioning Job about his knowledge of the power of God to save man from sin. Did Job know who measured out and planned to save mankind from sin? Did he know the Son of God would willingly come to earth as a man and shed His blood to free man from sin (John 10:17–18).

Then God asked:

Whereupon are the foundations thereof fastened? or who **laid the corner stone** thereof. (Job 38:6)

This is the only verse in the King James Version of the Bible where the Hebrew word *'eden* (as a sense of strength) is translated as "whereupon are the foundations." Fifty-five times *'eden* is used for the silver sockets made for the foundation of the Holy Place and the Holy of Holies in the tabernacle of Moses (Exodus 26:19– Numbers 4:32). Those sockets represented Christ, who is the firm foundation upon whom we place our faith (1 Corinthians 3:11). Jesus is also the cornerstone on whom the church of God is built (Isaiah 28:16; Ephesians 2:20).

The Hebrew word *'eden* is the name God gave to the place where He planted a garden. God put the man He had formed from the ground in Eden (Genesis 2:8), and it was in Eden, a place of God's strength, that Adam sinned.

The angels were singing for joy when God fastened the foundations of the earth, and laid its corner stone (Job 38:7).

Again God questions Job:

> Have the gates of death been opened unto thee? or
> hast thou seen the doors of the shadow of death?
> Hast thou perceived the breadth of the earth?
> declare if thou knowest it all. (Job 38:17–18)

Did Job know the darkness that covered the deep, or had he seen the gates of death. Did he know the size of the earth?

God continued questioning Job asking if he knew the way to where light lives. Or did he know the place of darkness? Did he know to which place (light or darkness) he was going? And how did he know this? Did he know because of the place where he was born or because of the number of years he had lived? (Job 38:19–21). With these questions God taught Job of His power over darkness, saving mankind from sin and death. It is the same lesson Moses learned when seeing God's glory. Moses wrote of this saying:

> The Spirit of God moved upon the face of the waters. And God said, Let there be light: and there was light. And God saw the light, that it was good: (Genesis 1:2–4)

The disciple John, having personally walked with Jesus, wrote "the light shineth in darkness; and the darkness comprehended it not." (John 1:5). Darkness will never comprehend (lay hold of, or take possession of) God's power, His knowledge, or His presence. Darkness has no power over the light, it has no knowledge that light does not have, and it cannot be present where there is light.

John, having personally known Jesus, began his gospel:

> In the beginning was the Word, and the Word was with God, and the Word was God. The same was in the beginning with God. (John 1:1–2)

And Moses said it this way:

> God divided the light from the darkness. And God called the light Day, and the darkness he called Night. (Genesis 1:4–5)

When a light is turned on in a dark room, the light extinguishes the darkness. But the darkness Moses saw was not extinguished when God said, "Let there be light." God divided the darkness (that which is unholy) from the light (that which is holy), and He saw that only the light was good.

> The evening and the morning were the first day. (Genesis 1:5)

HOW LONG WAS THE FIRST DAY?

We think of a day as a twenty-four-hour period of time determined by the Earth's rotation around the sun. However, because God did not make the sun until the fourth day (Genesis 1:14–19), the first day in Genesis cannot be defined by the sun.

From a scriptural point of view, a more accurate definition for a *day* would be the beginning and the end of an event that occurred within eternity. Only God knows when the first day began, but we know it ended when God called the light Day and the darkness Night.

Peter said that one day with the Lord God is like a thousand years and a thousand years like a day (2 Peter 3:8). Some see this as a prophetic warning, with each of the six days of Genesis representing one thousand years from the sin of Adam to the second coming of Jesus Christ, and the seventh day representing the one-thousand-year reign of Christ (Revelation 20:1-4). If that is the case, Jesus will certainly be coming soon.

God's word assures us Jesus is coming back again. Only God

the Father knows on which day He will return (Matthew 24:36–44). Today may not be the day Jesus returns, but it is the day for salvation in Christ Jesus (2 Corinthians 6:2).

The angels of God rejoiced and sang with shouts of joy when God fastened the earth's foundation and laid its cornerstone (Job 38:7). Luke said there is joy among the angels of God when one sinner repents (Luke 15:10).

JOB FINDS SALVATION

In the book of Job, from the thirty-eighth chapter to the forty-first chapter, God questioned Job. Then, with all his self-righteousness gone, in absolute defeat, Job said:

> Therefore have I uttered that I understood not;
> things too wonderful for me, which I knew not.
> (Job 42:3)

Job then humbly petitions God to hear him ... he is prepared to give God his answer.

This is Job's prayer of repentance that saved him from sin and death.

> I have heard of thee by the hearing of the ear:
> but now mine eye seeth thee. Wherefore I abhor
> [despise] myself, and repent in dust and ashes. (Job
> 42:5–6)

God promised the hope of eternal life before the world began

(Titus 1:2). Hope is not that God will save us from sin and death, He has. Hope is that we will receive salvation. "If we confess our sins, he is faithful and just to forgive us our sins, and to cleanse us from all unrighteousness" (1 John 1:9).

TRUSTING GOD'S WORD

The word *canon* refers to the criteria for determining which ancient writings were divinely inspired by God.

The canonical writings of the Old Testament required the authority of a spiritual leader. Prophets, kings, judges, priests, and scribes were the spiritual leaders of their time.

New Testament canonical writings are those of the original apostles or based on the testimony of an original apostle (such as Peter giving testimony to Paul's writings in 2 Peter 3:15).

The writings must be in agreement with the life of Jesus. He said: "These are the words which I spake unto you, while I was yet with you, that all things must be fulfilled, which were written in the law of Moses, and in the prophets, and in the psalms, concerning me." (Luke 24:44).

GOD IS OMNIPOTENT

Ah Lord God! behold, thou hast made the heaven and the earth by thy great power and stretched out arm, and there is nothing too hard for thee: (Jeremiah 32:17)

GOD IS OMNISCIENT

Hast thou not known? hast thou not heard, that the everlasting God, the Lord, the Creator of the ends of the earth, fainteth not, neither is weary? there is no searching of his understanding. (Isaiah 40:28)

GOD IS OMNIPRESENT

Will God indeed dwell on the earth? behold, the heaven and heaven of heavens cannot contain thee; how much less this house that I have builded? (1 Kings 8:27)

CHAPTER 3

DAY 2 – THE FIRMAMENT

Genesis 1:1 in the King James Version of the Bible reads: "In the beginning God created the *heaven* and the earth." Most modern translations read, "In the beginning God created the *heavens* and the earth." Which is right, singular or plural?

In the New Testament Stephen and Paul spoke of a third heaven. But in the beginning did God create one heaven, or multiple heavens? Let's go back to Stephen and Paul to find our answer.

After Jesus ascended into heaven His faithful followers were in the city of Jerusalem. They gathered together for a single purpose —they were waiting as Jesus instructed them, "until ye be endued with power from on high" (Luke 24:49).

Ten days after His ascension, a sound came from heaven and what looked like tongues of fire descended on each person there as they were filled with God's Holy Spirit (Acts 2:1–4).

Just as Jesus had promised, the people gathered together were empowered by the Holy Spirit of God. No longer afraid, they began telling others of Jesus Christ, whom God had raised from the dead (Romans 6:4) and now stands at the right hand of God. They warned people of their need to repent of sin and be baptized in the name of Jesus for the forgiveness of sin. As many as three thousand people were added to the church in one day (Acts 2:14–41).

With this rapidly growing church, the disciples chose seven honest men, all filled with God's Holy Spirit, to serve the needy. Stephen was one of those men. Being full of faith and power, he performed great miracles among the people (Acts 6:1–8).

In opposition to Stephen, a group of Jews caused riots among the people, with false accusations against him. Stephen was brought to trial before a council of high priests, where he was falsely accused of speaking lies against God, against Moses, against the law, and against the temple (Acts 6:9–15).

Stephen defended himself by acknowledging his belief in the faith and obedience of Abraham and Moses, and in God's law and His temple (Acts 7:1–50). Realizing that to say anything more would surely mean his death, he rightfully accused them of killing the prophets of God and resisting the Holy Spirit with their traditional beliefs (Acts 7:51–53).

Stephen hadn't said anything new, Jesus accused the scribes and Pharisees of transgressing the commandments of God with their traditional beliefs (Matthew 15:3).

Hearing Stephen's allegations against them, his accusers cursed at him, and Stephen "being full of the Holy Ghost, looked up stedfastly into heaven, and saw the glory of God, and Jesus standing on the right hand of God, and said, Behold, I see the heavens opened, and the Son of man standing on the right hand of God." (Acts 7:55–56).

When Stephen told them what he saw, they threw him out of the city and stoned him to death (Acts 7:57–58).

Present at Stephen's stoning was a man named Saul, a Pharisee who had consented to Stephen's death (Acts 8:1; 22:20).

Saul, whose Hebrew name means "desired," was highly educated in the Hebrew Scriptures. As a Pharisee he believed that their traditions were equal to the authority of Scripture (Philippians 3:5).

Shortly after Stephen's death, Saul miraculously encountered Jesus Christ while on his way to Damascus. Being blinded by that encounter, Saul was taken to Damascus. For three days he did not eat or drink anything until a man named Ananias, who was sent by God, prayed for Saul and he regained his sight. Saul then received the Holy Ghost and was water baptized (Acts 9:1–18).

After his conversion Saul traveled to Arabia before returning to Damascus. Three years later he went to Jerusalem where he stayed with Peter for fifteen days. During this time Saul did not meet any of the other apostles except James, Jesus's half-brother (Galatians 1:17–19).

Fourteen years later, because of a revelation he received from the Lord, Saul returned to Jerusalem with Barnabas and Titus. The apostles agreed that God had appointed Saul to proclaim the gospel to the Gentiles (Galatians 2:1–9).

Saul became a powerful witness to the glory and power of God for salvation through Jesus Christ. He began using his Roman name *Paul* because it was more favorable to the Gentiles (Acts 13:9).

This is one of the many revelations Paul received from God during his years of ministry.

> I knew a man in Christ above fourteen years ago, (whether in the body, I cannot tell; or whether out of the body, I cannot tell: God knoweth;) such an one caught up to the **third heaven**. And I knew such a man, (whether in the body, or out of the body, I cannot tell: God knoweth;) How that he was caught up into paradise, and heard unspeakable words, which it is not lawful for a man to utter. (2 Corinthians 12:2–4)

Paul was taken up to the very place where Stephen saw Jesus standing at the right hand of God, and he identified that place as the third heaven.

Let's go back to the first chapter of Genesis to learn more about the third heaven that Stephen saw and Paul visited. Keep in mind salvation is not seen in what God created (something new), but in the things God made (fashioned).

> God said, Let there be a firmament in the midst of the waters, and let it divide the waters from the waters. And **God made the firmament**, and divided the waters which were under the firmament

from the waters which were above the firmament:
and it was so. **And God called the firmament
Heaven**. And the evening and the morning were
the second day. (Genesis 1:6–8)

After God made (not created) the firmament, instead of there
being only the heaven and the earth as it was at creation, there
were now three heavens and one earth.

- The third heaven is above the firmament.
- The second heaven is the firmament.
- The first heaven is below the firmament.
- All three heavens are above the earth.

The King James Version of Genesis 1:1 is correct. In the
beginning God created one heaven. Bible translations agree that
at the end of the sixth day there were multiple heavens: "Thus the
heavens and the earth were finished, and all the host of them."
(Genesis 2:1).

This brings us to a key verse that Paul wrote pertaining to the
things God made.

> For (affirming) the invisible things of him from
> the creation of the world are clearly seen, **being
> understood by the things that are made**, even
> his eternal power and Godhead; so that they are
> without excuse: (Romans 1:20, brackets mine)

When Satan rebelled, God never restored the fallen angels

back to Himself. God, knowing Adam would sin, systematically began establishing His plan to save mankind from sin.

On the first day God said "Let there be light", and God divided the light from the darkness. On the second day God made the firmament, dividing the waters from the waters.

THE FIRMAMENT AND THE RED SEA

Three months after God divided the waters of the Red Sea, from the cleft of a rock, Moses saw God had made the firmament by dividing the waters above the earth (Exodus 19:1). The firmament was a type and shadow to the Exodus, just as the Exodus is a sign to salvation in Jesus Christ.

At the Exodus God led the Israelites on a very long journey, from Rameses to the Red Sea, in a pillar of cloud by day and a pillar of fire by night (Exodus 13:21), camping only twice.

First they camped at Succoth (Numbers 33:3–5). The second time was at Etham (Numbers 33:6). At Etham the Lord spoke to Moses, saying the people were to turn around and go back to Pihahiroth, or to the place where the sedge grows. Pharaoh would find them there and think they were shut in with nowhere to go. There everyone would know "I am the Lord" (Exodus 13:20–14:4; Numbers 33:6–8).

Having camped twice the Israelite were at Pihahiroth when God divided the waters of the Red Sea. All that night the Israelites crossed through the Red Sea on dry ground (Exodus 14:21–22). Because their day ended at sunset, having camped twice, it would seem the Israelites crossed through the Red Sea on the third day after eating the Passover meal.

It was during the morning watch when God confused the Egyptians by taking off their chariot wheels. God told Moses to stretch out his hand over the Red Sea, and when he did the sea returned to its depth drowning the Egyptians. Seeing what God had done the people feared the Lord, and believed the Lord and his servant Moses (Exodus 14:24–31).

Forty years later Joshua sent two men to spy out the land of Canaan, the land God promised to Abraham. While in the city of Jericho, Rahab hid them from the king's men saying, "For we have heard how the Lord dried up the water of the Red sea for you, when ye came out of Egypt; and what ye did unto the two kings of the Amorites, that were on the other side Jordan, Sihon and Og, whom ye utterly destroyed. And as soon as we had heard these things, our hearts did melt, neither did there remain any more courage in any man, because of you: for the Lord your God, he is God in heaven above, and in earth beneath." (Joshua 2:10–11).

Fifteen hundred years after the Exodus, on third day after eating the Passover meal, Jesus rose from the dead making a way for all people to cross over from death into everlasting life.

It was during the morning watch when the women went to Jesus' tomb and found it empty (Matthew 28:1–6; Mark 16:1–6; Luke 24:1–9; John 20:1–18). From the empty tomb we can know Jesus as our Lord.

Unlike Rehab, who feared the Lord, the chief priest paid the Roman soldiers guarding Jesus' tomb to say that during the night, while they were sleeping, the disciples came and stole His body (Matthew 28:11–15).

Paul said "if thou shalt confess with thy mouth the Lord Jesus, and shalt believe in thine heart that God hath raised him from the dead, thou shalt be saved. For with the heart man believeth unto righteousness; and with the mouth confession is made unto salvation" (Romans 10:9–10).

JESUS IS OUR GREAT HIGH PRIEST

Seeing then that we have a great high priest, that is passed into the heavens, Jesus the Son of God, let us hold fast our profession. (Hebrews 4:14)

GOD IS HOLY

Sanctify yourselves therefore, and be ye holy: for I am the Lord your God. And ye shall keep my statutes, and do them: I am the Lord which sanctify you. (Leviticus 20:7–8)

CHRIST, OUR PASSOVER

Purge out therefore the old leaven, that ye may be a new lump, as ye are unleavened. For even Christ our Passover is sacrificed for us: (1 Corinthians 5:7)

CHAPTER 4

DAY 3 – BROUGHT FORTH

In John's gospel we read the story of a Samaritan woman who went to the well outside the city Sychar to get water, and there she found Jesus resting from His journey. When Jesus asked the woman for a drink of water, she questioned why He, a Jewish man, would asked her, a Samaritan woman, for a drink. Jewish men considered it undignified for a man to talk to a woman in public, even to his wife, and the Jews had nothing to do with the Samaritans (John 4:1–9).

Jesus answered the woman, "If thou knewest the gift of God, and who it is that saith to thee, Give me to drink; thou wouldest have asked of him, and he would have given thee living water" (John 4:10).

Perceiving Jesus to be a prophet, she said, "I know that Messiah cometh, which is called Christ: when he is come, he will tell us all things" (John 4:25).

Jesus said, "I that speak unto thee am he" (John 4:26).

As soon as Jesus said this, His disciples returned from the city where they had gone to buy food. They too were surprised to see Jesus talking to a Samaritan woman.

She left her water jar, ran back into the city, and said, "Come, see a man, which told me all things that ever I did: is not this the Christ?" (John 4:29).

Surely the people of Sychar had heard stories of the many miracles Jesus had performed. When the Samaritan woman said she had met the man who performed those miracles, they came out to meet Him, and invited Him to stay with them.

Jesus spent two days with the people of Sychar.

> Many more believed because of his own word; and said unto the woman, Now we believe, not because of thy saying: for **we have heard him ourselves**, and know that this is indeed the Christ, the Savior of the world. (John 4:41–42)

An important lesson from the people of Sychar: faith comes by hearing the word of God.

THE LOGOS AND THE RHĒMA

The Greek words "logos" and "rhēma" are both translated "word" in the New Testament.

Logos is in reference to Jesus Christ the living word of God, and the inspired written word of God.

- "In the beginning was the Word, and the Word was with God, and the Word was God." (John 1:1)
- "For the word of God is quick, and powerful, and sharper than any twoedged sword, piercing even to the dividing asunder of soul and spirit, and of the joints and marrow, and is a discerner of the thoughts and intents of the heart." (Hebrews 4:12)

Rhēma means "utterance".

- "So then faith cometh by hearing, and hearing by the word of God" (Romans 10:17).
- "And take the helmet of salvation, and the sword of the Spirit, which is the word of God." (Ephesians 6:17).

The thirty nine canonical books of the Old Testament and all twenty seven books of the New Testament are the infallible, life giving, word of God. There are no contradictions — Scripture will always supports Scripture.

> The word of the Lord endureth for ever. And this is the word which by the gospel is preached unto you. (1Peter 1:25)

The word of God is both creative, and it is also life giving. Through the word of God the Holy Spirit "quickens", or gives life.

> I give thee charge in the sight of God, who **quickeneth** all things. (1 Timothy 6:13)

> Not by might, nor by power, but by my spirit, saith
> the Lord of hosts. (Zechariah 4:6)

BROUGHT FORTH

After God created the heaven and the earth, it was the word of God that brought forth life from the ground, on the third day when God said:

> Let the waters under the heaven be gathered together unto one place, and let the dry land appear: and it was so. **And God called the dry land Earth;** and the gathering together of **the waters called he Seas**. and God saw that it was good. (Genesis 1:9–10)

Every language has its own name for our planet, but they all are derived from a word meaning "ground or soil." Earth is the English/German word translated from the Hebrew *érets*. Throughout Scripture érets is also translated land, country, or world.

The problem with translating the dry land as "Earth" is that our planet includes both water and dry land, and God gave individual names and meaning to the dry land and the water. God called the dry land—ground.

On the third day God gathered the waters that covered the Earth so the dry land would appear, and God called the waters "seas". And God saw that it was good.

Throughout the Bible, *seas* speaks of the powerful voice of

God over the Earth and the multitude of people praising the Lord God (Psalm 29:3–4; Ezekiel 43:2; Revelation 1:15; 14:2; 19:6).

The third day continues with God saying:

> Let the earth [dry land] **bring forth** grass, the herb yielding seed, and the fruit tree yielding fruit after his kind, whose seed is in itself, upon the earth [dry land]: and it was so. (Genesis 1:11)

"Bring forth" refers to plants that grow, or sprout up from the dry land, giving special attention to the plants and trees that grow from seed. Bringing forth was not the creative work of God, it was the "quickening" work of God upon the dry land.

> And the earth [dry land] **brought forth** grass, and herb yielding seed after his kind, and the tree yielding fruit, whose seed was in itself, after his kind: and God saw that it was good. (Genesis 1:12)

In this verse "brought forth" means to come out, or to grow up out of the dry ground. The grass covers the pastures, and grazing animals like to eat it. The herb-yielding seed refers to plants that provide food for the human body. Trees are essential for the air we breathe, and they yield fruit whose seed is in itself.

> And the evening and the morning were the third day. (Genesis 1:13)

A PROFOUND TRUTH

God's power to bring forth, or to quicken, the spirit of man from death to life is revealed on the third day when God brought forth life from the dry land.

GOD CREATES A SPIRIT MAN

On the sixth day God created man (male and female) in His image and likeness—spirit beings. God blessed them and showed them the Earth. However, as spirit beings they could not move into their new home. God made it possible for them to live on the earth by giving them bodies to live in.

> The Lord God formed man of the dust of the ground, and breathed into his nostrils the breath of life; and man became a living soul. (Genesis 2:7)

Just as God changed Abram's name to Abraham, Sarai to Sarah, and Jacob to Israel, God changed the dry ground (érets) He formed man out of to *ádamah,* giving it a new identity. Ádamah is the Hebrew word for "ground or land" from where we get the name Adam. God breathed the male spirit He had created into the male body He formed, and gave him a soul; his mind, free will, and emotions.

Man, now living in a body of flesh and blood, was put in the garden that God planted in Eden, he was to work and care for it (Genesis 2:8). The female spirit had not yet been given a body, God gave this command only to Adam:

> Of every tree of the garden thou mayest freely eat:
> But of the tree of the knowledge of good and evil,
> thou shalt not eat of it: for in the day that thou eatest
> thereof thou shalt surely die. (Genesis 2:16–17)

Then God said it is not good for man to be alone. Instead of making a body for the woman, God formed every beast of the field and fowl of the air from the ground (also translated from the Hebrew *ádamah*, which is why animals share some of the same DNA as man), and God brought the animals to Adam for him to name (Genesis 2:18–19).

When Satan came to Adam disguised as an animal, Adam saw through his disguise and named this one *serpent*, which means subtle, shrewd, and crafty (Genesis 3:1).

After naming all the animals, Adam knew that none was a suitable partner for him to build a family with (Genesis 2:20).

> The Lord God caused a deep sleep to fall upon
> Adam, and he slept: and he took one of his ribs,
> and closed up the flesh instead thereof; and the rib,
> which the Lord God had taken from man, **made
> he a woman**, and brought her unto the man.
> (Genesis 2:21–22)

God did not form the woman from the dust of the ground, as He did the man. God made a body for the woman from the rib of man. The word "made" means "to begin to build a family." The woman, having a womb for Adam's seed, was a suitable partner for him. God brought the woman to Adam, and knowing they would have a family together, Adam said:

> This is now bone of my bones, and flesh of my flesh: she shall be called Woman [wife], because she was taken out of Man [husband]. (Genesis 2:23)

And God said:

> Therefore shall a man [husband] leave his father and his mother, and shall cleave unto his wife: and they shall be one flesh. (Genesis 2:24)

While in the garden Adam and the woman were in the presence of God and they could clearly hear His voice (Genesis 3:8).

DIVIDED FROM GOD

The woman, not recognizing the cunning liar disguised as a serpent, was the first to be deceived. Satan questioning her saying. "Hath God said, Ye shall not eat of every tree of the garden?" (Genesis 3:1). The woman, having knowledge of God's command, answered that they could eat of all the trees in the garden except one. They were not to even touch the tree in the middle of the garden or they would die (Genesis 3:2–3).

The serpent lied to her, saying, "Ye shall not surely die" (Genesis 3:4).

Then the serpent told her the truth. "God doth know that in

the day ye eat thereof, then your eyes shall be opened, and ye shall be as gods, knowing good and evil" (Genesis 3:5).

The woman ate the fruit from the tree of the knowledge of good and evil. Then she gave the fruit to Adam, and when he ate "the eyes of them both were opened, and they knew that they were naked" (Genesis 3:7).

Disobeying God's command, Adam and Eve alienated themselves from God. Their heart (spirit) now darkened, and living without the law, they were ignorant of knowing how to live in holiness to God (Ephesians 4:18).

Because of Adam's sin their body, which had eternal life, began to die. And still today when the body dies it returns to dust (Genesis 3:19). Adam's body died nine hundred and thirty years after he sinned (Genesis 5:5).

Covering their nakedness with fig leaves, Adam and the woman hid from the presence of the Lord God among the trees of the garden (Genesis 3:7–8). Never before had they felt afraid (Genesis 3:10).

God could have destroyed Adam and the woman and formed another man, and another, and another. But knowing that all men would sin and fall short of His glory (Romans 3:23), and having planned for the salvation of mankind, God said to the serpent:

> I will put enmity [hatred] between thee and the woman, and between thy seed and **her seed**; it shall bruise thy head, and thou shalt bruise his heel. (Genesis 3:15)

God didn't say this for the serpent to hear, Satan already knew he was powerless against God. God said this for Adam and the woman to hear so they would know that one day God would restore mankind to Himself.

After sinning Adam named his wife Eve, saying she would be the mother of all the living (Genesis 3:20).

God made the first animal sacrifice, and used its blood as a temporary covering over man's sin. God made leather clothes for Adam and Eve (Genesis 3:21)

To keep them from being eternally separated from Him, God sent them out of the garden and placed Cherubims, and a flaming sword to guard the way to the tree life (Genesis 3:22–24).

When Adam sinned his seed was genetically altered from sinless to sinful. Because the human race traces back to Adam, every person — with the exception of Jesus Christ who was not born from the seed of a man (Luke 1:26–35) — is born spiritually separated from God.

> As by one man sin entered into the world, and death by sin; and so death passed upon all men, for that all have sinned. (Romans 5:12)

Because the woman was taken from Adam's rib she became sin when he sinned. However, it is through the seed of Adam that all men are born sinners, and not from the womb of the woman.

Jesus Christ wasn't born from the seed of a man, but from the womb of a sinful woman he was born a sinless man. Jesus Christ is the Son of God and the son of man.

If through the offence of one [Adam] many be dead, much more the grace of God, and the gift by grace, which is by one man, Jesus Christ, hath abounded unto many. (Romans 5:15).

Every person is eternally known by God. God thought of you before He created you. Thoughts of peace and not of calamity. He planned for each person's future, and God gives each person hope for their future. God's hope is that every person will call upon Him, pray to Him and seek Him with all their heart. From heaven He will hear them and they would find Him, then God will save them from sin (Jeremiah 29:11–14).

WHAT IS SALVATION

Through faith in Jesus Christ our spirit is brought forth from sin (death) and made sinless (alive). Salvation is not a creative work of God, it is God quickening, or bringing forth, the spirit of man from death to life. Salvation is the rebirth of our spirit.

The mind is not quickened like our spirit is. The mind is made new, transformed, by learning and speaking the word of God.

Jesus prayed:

Sanctify [purify] them through thy truth: thy word [logos] is truth (John 17:17)

Be not conformed to this world: but be ye transformed by the renewing of your mind, that ye may prove what is that good, and acceptable, and perfect, will of God." (Romans 12:2).

WHEN CAN A PERSON BE SAVED

This is the day of salvation. If today you hear His voice, do not harden your heart (Psalm 95:7–8).

> I have heard thee in a time accepted, and in the day of salvation have I succoured [helped] thee: behold, now is the accepted time; behold, **now is the day of salvation**. (2 Corinthians 6:2)

HOW IS SALVATION RECEIVED

Paul and Silas were in Macedonia, by a river outside the city of Philippi, speaking to the women who had gathered to pray. Lydia, who worshipped God, was there. Hearing Paul and Silas the Lord opened her heart. She and her household believing in God were saved, and baptized (Acts 16:12–15).

While in Philippi, Paul and Silas were thrown into prison for preaching the gospel, which was contrary to Roman law and customs. At midnight Paul and Silas were praying and praising God when suddenly there was an earthquake. The prison doors opened, and the prisoners were freed from their chains. The prison guard, supposing the prisoners had fled, was about to kill himself when Paul called out to stop him. Realizing no prisoner had escaped, the prison guard asked Paul and Silas "what must I do to be saved?", and they said "Believe on the Lord Jesus Christ" (Acts

16:16–31). The guard brought Paul and Silas to his home where he and his family believed in God and were baptized (Acts 16:32–34).

Jesus said "Verily, verily, I say unto thee, Except a man be born again, he cannot see the kingdom of God" (John 3:3).

> Being born again, not of corruptible seed, but of incorruptible, by the word of God, which liveth and abideth for ever. (1 Peter 1:23)

"In this was manifested the love of God toward us, because that God sent his only begotten Son into the world, that we might live through him. Herein is love, not that we loved God, but that he loved us, and sent his Son to be the propitiation [the means of appeasing] for our sins." (1 John 4:9–10)

AFTER THE BODY DIES

When the heart stops beating the body dies, and it will eventually return to dust. However, our spirit and soul live on for all eternity.

Those having accepted Jesus will live on to everlasting life, inheriting all good things with God as their Father (Revelation 21:6–7).

Those having rejected Jesus by not receiving salvation will live on to shame and everlasting contempt (Daniel 12:2–3; Revelation 20:12–15).

Salvation is a personal choice, and only God can see into the "heart" of a person. God knows the thoughts we think, what our intentions are, and what motivates us. Man looks at the outward appearance, but God looks at the heart (1 Samuel 16:7).

JESUS IS EMMANUEL

Behold, a virgin shall be with child, and shall bring forth a son, and they shall call his name Emmanuel, which being interpreted is, God with us. (Matthew 1:23)

JESUS IS THE CHRIST

Peter said unto them, Repent, and be baptized every one of you in the name of Jesus Christ for the remission of sins, and ye shall receive the gift of the Holy Ghost. (Acts 2:38)

GOD IS MY DWELLING PLACE

He that dwelleth in the secret place of the most High shall abide under the shadow of the Almighty. I will say of the Lord, He is my refuge and my fortress: my God; in him will I trust. (Psalm 91:1–2)

CHAPTER 5

DAY 4 – TWO GREAT LIGHTS

The lights of the fourth day are different from the light on the first day.

- The light on the first day is singular. On the fourth day God made two great lights.
- The light on the first day did not have boundaries. On the fourth day the lights were set in the firmament of heaven.
- On the first day God divided light (life) from darkness (death). On the fourth day the lights divided the day from the night.
- The light on the first day was salvation. The lights on the fourth day included signals to the seasons, days, and years for salvation.
- On the first day God saw the light was good. On the fourth day God saw the lights were good.

Referring to the light of the first day, John wrote, "In him [Jesus] was life; and the life was the light of men" (John 1:4)

It is not a coincidence that John begins his gospel at the very same place Moses began the book of Genesis:

> In the beginning was the Word, and the Word was with God, and the Word was God. The same was in the beginning with God. **All things were made by him; and without him was not any thing made that was made.** (John 1:1–3)

On the fourth day God made (not created) the two great lights.

> And God said, Let there be lights in the firmament of the heaven to divide the day from the night; and **let them be for signs, and for seasons, and for days, and years**: and let them be for lights in the firmament of the heaven to give light upon the earth: and it was so. (Genesis 1:14–15)

The word translated *years* is the Hebrew word *shaneh*. In the Bible it is used to define a division of time, a lifetime, or a revolution of time. The English word *revolution* is an alternative word for violence, rebellion, revolt, uprising, mutiny and upheaval, which well describes the place in eternity from where God began to show Moses His glory. When God made the two great lights, He set the number of days that this revolt against Him would last.

God **made** two great lights; the greater light to rule the day, and the lesser light to rule the night: he **made** the stars also. And God set them in the firmament of the heaven to give light upon the earth, and to rule over the day and over the night, and to divide the light from the darkness: and God saw that it was good. And the evening and the morning were the fourth day. (Genesis 1:16–19)

Tradition has it that on the fourth day God created the sun, moon, and stars. Yet the words *created*, *sun*, and *moon* are not found within any of these verses. On the fourth day God "made two great lights".

Referring to the sun, moon, and stars, Paul wrote:

There is one glory of the sun, and another glory of the moon, and another glory of the stars: for one star differeth from another star in glory. (1 Corinthians 15:41)

THE GREATER LIGHT

Of the two great lights, the greater light to rule the day is obviously the sun. Because the sun gives light to the Earth, it can be compared to Jesus, who is the Light of the world, from whom we receive the light of life (John 8:12). Because the sun is a ball of fire it is also reminds us of the final judgment, and the fate of those who reject Jesus. (Revelation 20:11–15; 21:8).

THE LESSER LIGHT

Some may think the moon is the "lesser light to rule the night". But the moon has no light of its own; it reflects the light of the sun. Look again at Genesis 1:16:

> God made two great lights; the greater light to rule the day, and the lesser light to rule the night: he made the stars also.

One of the difficulties in translating Scripture was that in ancient times it was customary for Hebrew and Greek manuscripts to be written with few if any punctuation marks. In the King James Version of the Bible, the italicized words were added to bring clarity to the reader.

Genesis 1:16 without the punctuation marks and the added words, would read:

> God made two great lights the greater light to rule the day and the lesser light to rule the night the stars also.

Unlike the moon, stars have their own light, which makes them the "lesser light to rule the night."

God compared the redeemed of the Lord to the number of stars, saying to Abraham, "Look now toward heaven, and tell the stars, if thou be able to number them: and he said unto him, So shall thy seed be" (Genesis 15:5).

After the birth of Jesus, a star led the magi to Jerusalem, and their arrival so alarmed King Herod that he demanded his chief priest and scribes tell him where Christ was prophesied to be born. The magi were called to meet with Herod privately, and he sent them to Bethlehem, again being led by the star (Matthew 2:1–10).

Jesus, the Son of God, became the Son of Man, and a star was seen across the night sky as a sign of His birth.

"Praise ye him, sun and moon: praise him, all ye stars of light" (Psalm 148:3).

THE MOON

In addition to the two great lights, God made the moon. The moon is for signs, seasons, and days.

More than a thousand years before God sent Moses and Aaron to Egypt, the Egyptians used what was mainly a solar calendar, and the sun was a god to the Egyptians. The primary name for the sun god of ancient Egypt was Ra. The Israelites living in Egypt would have known only the Egyptian solar calendar.

God prepared Moses and Aaron for the first Passover by giving them His calendar, a lunar calendar, with the moon signaling when God's feast days were to be celebrated. God said to them: "This month shall be unto you the beginning of months: it shall be the first month of the year to you" (Exodus 12:2). God told them on which days His feast of Passover and Unleavened Bread were to be celebrated (Exodus 12:3–17).

Moses was back on Mount Sinai when God gave him five additional feast days, also to be celebrated yearly as memorials to the Lord throughout the generations (Exodus 12:14; Leviticus 23).

God gave Moses His eighth feast day when giving the Israelites manna (Exodus 16:23). The Sabbath, was to be celebrated weekly.

Here is a quick summary of God's eight feast days and how they relate to God's plan of redemption.

PASSOVER

Passover was celebrated in the first month, on the fourteenth day. At sunset, Passover began with the killing of a sacrificial lamb (Exodus 12:1–14).

Keep in mind, the fourteenth of the month does not fall on the same day of the week every year. God's first five feast days are specific to the year Jesus was crucified. That year the fourteenth day of the first month (Passover) fell on the fifth day of the week, the day we call Thursday.

Passover is a reflection of Jesus, the Lamb of God, who shed His blood to pay the penalty for all sin.

UNLEAVENED BREAD

At sunset, as the fourteenth day ended the fifteenth day began, and so did the seven-day feast of Unleavened Bread. During this feast the people ate bread made without yeast, which represented a life without sin (Exodus 12:15–20).

Jesus was crucified on the first day of the Feast of Unleavened bread. "He hath made him to be sin for us, who knew no sin; that we might be made the righteousness of God in him" (2 Corinthians 5:21).

On the sixth day of the week, the day we call Friday, God

created man. Four thousand years after Adam sinned, on the sixth day Jesus died to save man from sin.

SABBATH

The Sabbath is the only day to have both a number and a name. In Genesis, God having finished His work rested on the seventh day. The number seven represents the complete work of God. The name *Sabbath* signifies there is nothing man can do to add to the work that God has done.

God sent manna from heaven to the Israelites saying "To morrow is the rest of the holy sabbath unto the Lord" (Exodus 16:23), "Six days ye shall gather it; but on the seventh day, which is the sabbath, in it there shall be none" (Exodus 16:26). God commanded that anyone found working on the Sabbath, even to gather sticks, be stoned to death (Numbers 15:33–36). Jesus said, "Verily, verily, I say unto you, Moses gave you not that bread from heaven; but my Father giveth you the true bread from heaven. For the bread of God is he which cometh down from heaven, and giveth life unto the world. Then said they unto him, Lord, evermore [at all times] give us this bread. And Jesus said unto them, I am the bread of life: he that cometh to me shall never hunger; and he that believeth on me shall never thirst" (John 6:32–35).

Salvation is a work only God can do: "For by grace are ye saved through faith; and that not of yourselves: it is the gift of God: not of works, lest any man should boast" (Ephesians 2:8–9).

Jesus, having finished His work on the cross, was in the tomb on the Sabbath; the day we call Saturday. It was the second day of the Feast of Unleavened Bread.

The tradition of the first day of the week (Sunday) as a day for rest is not biblical. It was imposed on Christianity through a civil law issued by Constantine when he was emperor of Rome.

FEAST OF FIRST FRUITS

During the seven-day feast of Unleavened Bread, the Feast of First Fruits was to be celebrated on the first day after the Sabbath. It was a day to thank God for all of His provisions (Leviticus 23:10–11).

Jesus said, "Destroy this temple, and in three days I will raise it up" (John 2:19). On the third day after Passover Jesus rose from the dead, on the Feast of First Fruits.

"But now is Christ risen from the dead, and become the first-fruits of them that slept. For since by man came death, by man came also the resurrection of the dead. For as in Adam all die, even so in Christ shall all be made alive. But every man in his own order: Christ the firstfruits; afterward they that are Christ's at his coming" (1 Corinthians 15:20–23).

The Feast of First Fruits was celebrated on the first day after the Sabbath (Leviticus 23:11), the day we call Sunday.

FEAST OF WEEKS

The Feast of Weeks was celebrated fifty days after the Feast of First Fruits (Leviticus 23:15–16). In the New Testament the Feast of Weeks is called Pentecost, which is the Greek word for "the fiftieth day."

On the fiftieth day after Jesus rose from the dead, those gathered in Jerusalem waiting for the Father's promise were filled with God's Holy Spirit (Acts 2:1–4). Pentecost marked the beginning of the church age.

The last three of God's feast days have not yet been fulfilled. They celebrate the second coming of Jesus Christ, His one-thousand-year reign, and the redeemed living eternally in a messianic kingdom.

FEAST OF TRUMPETS

The Feast of Trumpets was celebrated on the first day of the seventh month (Leviticus 23:24) with the sound of a trumpet calling all people to repentance. The Feast of Trumpets celebrates the second coming of Jesus Christ and will be fulfilled with the rapture of all who have received salvation in Christ Jesus.

> In a moment, in the twinkling of an eye, at the last trump: for the trumpet shall sound, and the dead shall be raised incorruptible, and we shall be changed. For this corruptible must put on incorruption, and this **mortal must put on immortality**. (1 Corinthians 15:52–53)

The prophet Joel said "Blow ye the trumpet in Zion, and sound an alarm in my holy mountain: **let all the inhabitants of the land tremble**: for the day of the LORD cometh, for it is nigh at hand. (Joel 2:1) There is no place on earth where the sound of the final trumpet will not be heard.

DAY OF ATONEMENT

The Day of Atonement, also known as Yom Kippur, is celebrated on the tenth day of the seventh month (Leviticus 23:27). It is the holiest day of the year. It was the only day of the year that the high priest was allowed to enter the Holy of Holies, and only with the blood of a lamb as atonement for the sins of the people.

The Day of Atonement marks the end of the years of rebellion against God and the end of God's grace for salvation. On this day the names of the redeemed are sealed in the Lamb's Book of Life.

FEAST OF TABERNACLES

The Feast of Tabernacles began on the fifteenth day of the seventh month. It signifies the redeemed living in a new heaven and a new earth in the shelter of God (Leviticus 23:34).

Together, God's seven yearly feast days are a full disclosure of the perfect and complete work of God for our salvation … as are the seven days of Genesis.

THE CALENDAR

In 46 BC the Roman calendar was replaced with the Julian calendar, named after Julius Caesar. In 1582 the Julian calendar was replaced by the Gregorian calendar, introduced by and named after Pope Gregory VIII. Still today people around the world rely on the Gregorian calendar to keep track of time.

Leap year is proof that our method of measuring time according to seconds, minutes, hours, and days is not exact to the Earth's orbit around the sun. No one has ever been able to measure time to the exactness of God when He created and made the universe.

As God planned, the week still consist of seven days, but the days that God numbered are now named. During the Hellenistic period (from the death of Alexander the Great in 323 BC to the rise of the Roman Empire in 31 BC) five of the seven days were named after planets, and then adopted by the Romans. Their English names are derived from mythological and legendary gods: Tuesday, a god of war; Wednesday, a supreme god; Thursday, a god thunder; Friday represents love and beauty. The seventh day, the only day God named, was named Saturday from Saturn, the ancient Roman god of fun and feasting.

The Emperor Constantine declared throughout the Roman Empire the "Venerable Day of the Sun," which is where we get the name Sunday. Monday is named after the moon.

The origin of the Gregorian calendar is that of a solar calendar on which time is measured in a linear, progressive manner.

The origin of the Hebrew calendar traces back to the lunar calendar God gave to Moses. Time is viewed as an ascending spiral, with repeated patterns or cycles that present a theme or revelation of sacred history.

The Milky Way galaxy is a spiral-shaped galaxy ... an illustration of God's divine plan and His appointed days.

Every sunrise and sunset also exemplifies "To day if ye will hear his voice, harden not your heart, as in the provocation [rebellion]" (Psalm 95:7–8; Hebrews 3:15).

"Let us therefore fear, lest, a promise being left us of entering

into his rest, any of you should seem to come short of it"
(Hebrews 4:1).

GOD IS THE DAY STAR

We have also a more sure word of prophecy;
whereunto ye do well that ye take heed, as unto
a light that shineth in a dark place, until the day
dawn, and the day star arise in your hearts: knowing
this first, that no prophecy of the scripture is of any
private interpretation. For the prophecy came not
in old time by the will of man: but holy men of
God spake as they were moved by the Holy Ghost.
(2 Peter 1:19 –21)

GOD IS THE FATHER OF LIGHTS

Every good gift and every perfect gift is from
above, and cometh down from the Father of lights,
with whom is no variableness, neither shadow of
turning. (James 1:17)

JESUS IS THE LIGHT OF THE WORLD

Then spake Jesus again unto them, saying, I am the
light of the world: he that followeth me shall not
walk in darkness, but shall have the light of life.
(John 8:12)

CHAPTER 6

DAY 5 – ANCIENT OF DAYS

Simon and his wife lived near the Sea of Galilee, where he made his living as a fisherman along with his partners James and John, the sons of Zebedee. When Simon's brother Andrew introduced him to Jesus, Jesus changed his name to Peter, saying, "Thou art Simon the son of Jona: thou shalt be called Cephas" (John 1:42), which in the Greek is Peter.

Unlike Andrew, Simon was not quick to follow Jesus. He had fished all night and was washing his nets when Jesus stepped onto his ship. Jesus asked Simon to take Him a little way out onto the water, away from the shore, so He could better teach the people. And Simon did.

When Jesus finished speaking to the people, He asked Simon to put out his nets for a catch of fish. Although he had fished all night and didn't catching anything, Simon let down his nets. They filled with such an abundance of fish that Simon called for James and John to come help him. Together they filled both ships so that they began to sink.

"When Simon Peter saw it, he fell down at Jesus' knees, saying, Depart from me; for I am a sinful man, O Lord" (Luke 5:8). That day Simon Peter, James, and John left everything and followed Jesus.

Sometime later Jesus asked His disciples, "Whom say ye that I am?" (Matthew 16:15)

Peter answered, "Thou art the Christ, the Son of the living God." (Matthew 16:16)

Jesus said, "Blessed art thou, Simon Barjona [son of Jona]: for flesh and blood hath not revealed it unto thee, but my Father which is in heaven. And I say also unto thee, that thou art Peter, and upon this rock I will build my church; and the gates of hell shall not prevail against it" (Matthew 16:17–18).

Before his death in 68 AD Peter wrote a letter to the believers in Jesus Christ. He warns that in the last days there will be false teachers — those who desire the things that God forbids. Peter encouraged all believers to be a witness to the gospel of Jesus Christ, and to remember what was spoken by the prophets of God (2 Peter 3:1–3). Surely one of the holy prophets Peter was referring to was Daniel, who in a night vision, learned of future events and saw the Ancient of Days (Daniel 7:9–14, 22). Daniel saw "there shall be a time of trouble, such as never was since there was a nation even to that same time: and at that time thy people shall be delivered, every one that shall be found written in the book. And many of them that sleep in the dust of the earth shall awake, some to everlasting life, and some to shame and everlasting contempt" (Daniel 12:1–2).

Jesus Himself said that just as there was tribulation at the beginning of the world, a great tribulation is yet to come.

> For then shall be great tribulation, such as was not since the beginning of the world to this time, no, nor shall ever be. And except those days should be shortened, there should no flesh be saved: but for the elect's sake those days shall be shortened. (Matthew 24:21–22)

God is the Alpha and the Omega, the beginning and the end (Revelation 1:8; 1:11; 21:6; 22:13). Moses saw God's glory from when salvation began, and Daniel from when salvation comes to an end. All the days of this heaven and earth are designed for the glory of God in saving man from sin and death.

PREHISTORIC EVENTS

Prehistoric relates to a time before written records were kept on Earth, but does not apply to the books in heaven (1 John 5:7; Revelation 5:1). Like Daniel, John also saw the books in heaven. "And I saw the dead, small and great, stand before God; and the books were opened: and another book was opened, which is the book of life: and the dead were judged out of those things which were written in the books, according to their works" (Revelation 20:12).

Other than the writings of Moses, we have only theories as to how God restored the Earth from when it was formless and void. Here is a comparison of the writing of Moses to some of those theories:

- *Moses*: God created the heaven and the Earth.
  Scientific theory: Heaven is 13.7 billion years old and the Earth is 4.5 billion years old (agreeing that heaven is older than the Earth).
- *Moses*: The Earth was without form and void.
  Scientific theory: The Earth was formless and covered in boiling liquid rock.
- *Moses*: God said, "Let there be light". Just as there was darkness over the land and the Earth quaked when Jesus died (Matthew 27:45–51), there would have been signs in heaven and on Earth when God said, "Let there be light".
  Scientific theory: Most researchers believe the Earth was formed by a series of meteorites that collided with the Earth.
- *Moses*: God made the firmament.
  Scientific theory: The liquid rock cooled and the iron settled to the Earth's core, resulting in a magnetic field above the Earth.
- *Moses*: The waters gathered together and dry land appeared.
  Scientific theory: How the Earth came to be covered in water is a great mystery.
- *Moses*: Vegetation was brought forth, and plants and trees grew.

Scientific theory: Life existed on the Earth billions of years ago, as indicated by fossils called stromatolites.

- *Moses*: God made two great lights to divide the day from the night and for signs, seasons, days, and years.
Scientific theory: The sun and the moon are about as old as the Earth.

This brings us to the fifth day in Genesis.

> God said, Let the waters bring forth abundantly the moving creature that hath life, and fowl that may fly above the earth in the open firmament of heaven. And God **created great whales**, and every living creature that moveth, which the waters brought forth abundantly, after their kind, and every winged fowl after his kind: and God saw that it was good. And God blessed them, saying, Be fruitful, and multiply, and fill the waters in the seas, and let fowl multiply in the earth. And the evening and the morning were the fifth day. (Genesis 1:20–23)

PREHISTORIC CREATURES

In Genesis 1:21 the word translated *great* is the same Hebrew word used in Genesis 1:16 for the great and greater lights. This is the only verse in the King James Version of the Bible where the word *whales* is found. (Jonah was swallowed by a "great fish").

Science agrees with Scripture, the waters first brought forth abundantly the moving creatures that hath life. The prehistoric creatures first lived in the seas, then on land and in the air.

"Whales" is translated from the Hebrew word *tanniyn* which is also translated as "serpent" (referring to Aaron's rod in Exodus 7:9–12, not the serpent in the garden who tempted Eve), "dragon" or "sea monster".

In Scripture the Hebrew word *tanniyn* is never translated to the familiar *dinosaur*. When my grandson Wyatt was eight years old he was interested in dinosaurs. He learned the names of many types, and was excited to show me pictures from his book of their skeletal forms. I believe on the fifth day Moses was writing about these prehistoric creatures that God created.

Many cultures throughout the world have legends of a "dragon". These tales fit the description of the creature God called Leviathan. It had scales, which were his pride, and out of his mouth came fire and from his nostrils smoke (Job 41:15–21). Because archeologists have not discovered any skeletal remains of a dragon, Leviathan is believed to be a myth. When God questioned Job about the creatures He referred to as "behemoth" and "leviathan" (Job 40:14–41:34), He identified them as Satan and his followers, the cause of Job's troubles (Job 42:1–6). Some people believe these demonic fallen angels are also myths.

SCOFFERS

Not only did Peter say we should remember what the holy prophets wrote, he also said we are to avoid scoffers—those who teach contrary to the word of God. Peter warned in the last days many will live recklessly and proud, lovers of pleasures more than lovers of God (2 Timothy 3:1-4). The prophet Isaiah said "Woe unto them that call evil good, and good evil; that put darkness for light, and light for darkness; that put bitter for sweet, and sweet for bitter!" (Isaiah 5:20). Peter called anyone who does not believe that this heaven and earth are reserved by God for the day of judgement, and the destruction of ungodly — willingly ignorant (2 Peter 3:3–7).

OVERCOMERS AND UNBELIEVERS

There will never be a day when mankind does not exist. God created man (male and female) spirit beings giving them eternal life … a life without end.

However, there will be "a new heaven and a new earth: for the first heaven and the first earth were passed away; and there was no more sea" (Revelation 21:1).

Those who find victory over sin and death through faith in Jesus Christ are the overcomers. "He that overcometh shall inherit all things; and I will be his God, and he shall be my son" (Revelation 21:7).

Those who did not find their victory in Jesus Christ, the fearful and unbelieving who spent their life on Earth in sin, shall have their destiny in the lake of fire (Revelation 21:8).

INHERITING THE KINGDOM OF GOD

The apostle Paul made it known that he was not sent to baptize, but to preach the gospel of the cross of Christ. A gospel that is foolishness to those who are perishing. But those who believe in the cross of Jesus Christ — they are saved from sin and death by the power of God (1 Corinthians 1:17–18).

Paul also said "Be not conformed to this world: but be ye transformed by the renewing of your mind, that ye may prove what is that good, and acceptable, and perfect, will of God." (Romans 12:2).

ANCIENT OF DAYS

I saw in the night visions, and, behold, one like the Son of man came with the clouds of heaven, and came to the Ancient of days, and they brought him near before him. And there was given him dominion, and glory, and a kingdom, that all people, nations, and languages, should serve him: his dominion is an everlasting dominion, which shall not pass away, and his kingdom that which shall not be destroyed. (Daniel 7:13–14)

GOD IS ETERNAL

Before the mountains were brought forth, or ever thou hadst formed the earth and the world, even from everlasting to everlasting, thou art God. (Psalm 90:2)

GOD IS TRUTH

But thou, O Lord, art a God full of compassion, and gracious, longsuffering, and plenteous in mercy and truth. (Psalm 86:15)

CHAPTER 7

DAY 6 – THE BLOOD

Paul was a highly educated man. Rabbi Gamaliel had taught him the Scriptures "according to the perfect manner of the law" (Acts 22:3). After his conversion he was tasked with taking the gospel of Jesus Christ to the Gentiles.

As an appointed preacher, apostle, and teacher to the Gentiles (2 Timothy 1:11) Paul didn't preach and teach the word as the learned men of his day. Paul shared the gospel from what he had received "by the revelation of Jesus Christ" (Galatians 1:12). He spoke "not with enticing words of man's wisdom, but in demonstration of the Spirit and of power: That your faith should not stand in the wisdom of men, but in the power of God" (1 Corinthians 2:4–5).

As a mentor to Timothy, and perceiving the Holy Spirit at work in his life, Paul advised him to "study to shew thyself approved unto God, a workman that needeth not to be ashamed, rightly dividing the word of truth." (2 Timothy 2:15).

The book of Galatians is the only letter Paul wrote to multiple churches, "unto the churches of Galatia" (Galatians 1:2). He accused those who were preaching the Law of Moses has the power over sin of perverting the gospel of Jesus Christ (Galatians 1:7). Having been sent by God to preach the gospel of Jesus Christ Paul said "Now to Abraham and his seed were the promises made. He saith not, And to seeds, as of many; but as of one, And to thy seed, which is Christ" (Galatians 3:16).

Paul consistently preached salvation came through the promises God gave to Abraham. God promised him that if he would leave his home land God would make him into a great nation, and he would become a blessing. In him all the families of the earth would be blessed. (Genesis 12:1–3). "There shall come out of Sion the Deliverer, and shall turn away ungodliness from Jacob: for this is my covenant unto them, when I shall take away their sins" (Romans 11:26–27).

Paul said God's promises were given to Abraham 430 years before He gave the law to Moses (Galatians 3:17). Moses said it was exactly 430 years, to the day, from the day God gave His promises to Abraham to the day he led the Israelites out of Egypt (Exodus 12:41).

The 430 years between the covenant (promise) and the law are confirmed in the genealogy from Abraham to Joseph. The Israelites were in Egypt for 215 of the 430 years, and of those years, after Joseph's death, they were treated as slaves for eighty years.

- Abram left his homeland when he was seventy-five years old (Genesis 12:4). He lived in Canaan for ten years before Sarah gave her Egyptian maid Hagar to him (Genesis 16:3). Abram was eighty-six years old when Ishmael was born (Genesis 16:16).
- Thirteen years later, Abraham was ninety-nine when God made covenant with him through Isaac, making the people of Israel God's chosen people. (Genesis 17:1–21).
- One year later Isaac was born (Genesis 21:5).
- Sixty years later Jacob was born to Isaac and Rebekah (Genesis 25:26).
- One-hundred and thirty years later Jacob moved his family to Egypt (Genesis 47:9).

This accounts for 215 of the 430 years.

- Seventeen years after moving to Egypt Jacob died (Genesis 47:28).
  a. Jacob's son Joseph was thirty years old when the seven years of plenty followed by seven years of famine began (Genesis 41:46).
  b. There were five years of famine yet to come when Jacob moved his family to Egypt (Genesis 45:6). This means Joseph was thirty-nine years old when Jacob moved to Egypt, and ninety-one years younger than his father Jacob.
- Fifty-four years later Joseph died at the age of 110 (Genesis 50:26).

This accounts for 286 of the 430 years, leaving 144 years unaccounted for.

After Joseph's death the Israelites were fruitful and increased abundantly because of what Joseph had done for Egypt (Exodus 1:7–8).

Moses's brother Aaron was three years older than Moses (Exodus 7:7), and his life was not threatened by the king's order to kill all Hebrew baby boys (Exodus 1:16). When Moses was born, by order of the king, he was to be killed (Exodus 2:1–10). This would mean that:

- Sixty-four years after Joseph died the Israelites were not oppressed.
- For eighty years, from when Moses was born until God sent him to Egypt, the Israelites were treated harshly.

This accounts for all 430 years. (The 400 years of Israel's affliction (Genesis 15:13) began when Ishmael mocked Isaac.)

Paul understood God's covenant promises to Abraham were for salvation, and he knew God's eternal power for salvation can be "clearly seen, being understood by the things that are made" (Romans 1:20).

THE SIXTH DAY

God said, Let the earth bring forth the living creature after his kind, cattle, and creeping thing, and beast of the earth after his kind: and it was so. And God **made** the beast of the earth after his kind, and cattle after their kind, and every thing that creepeth upon the earth after his kind: **and God saw that it was good**. (Genesis 1:24–25)

God's law would require the shedding of blood for the forgiveness of sin (Hebrews 9:22). On the sixth day, knowing Adam would sin, God made the beast of the earth — a blood covering for the sins of man. And God saw that it was good.

Throughout the Old Testament the blood of animals was a temporary substitutional covering over the sins of man.

After Adam sinned, and while still in the garden, God made the first animal sacrifice when He made coats of animal skin to clothe Adam and Eve before sending them out of the garden of Eden (Genesis 3:21).

Adam and Eve's son Abel was a keeper of sheep, and God respected Abel's sin offering of the firstborn of his flock (Genesis 4:2–4).

After the flood, Noah built an altar on which he placed burnt offerings to the Lord (Genesis 8:20–21).

The covenant God cut with Abraham was sealed with the blood of an animal. The law God gave to Moses was sprinkled with the blood of an animal. Within the tabernacle and the temple there was an altar for animal sacrifices, and their blood covered the sins of men.

The blood sacrifices of the Old Testament were done away with when Jesus shed His blood on the cross. The blood of Jesus did not temporarily cover over sin, Jesus is "the Lamb of God, which taketh away the sin of the world" (John 1:29). God demonstrated

His love for us in that while we were yet sinners Christ died to free us from sin and death (Romans 5:8–9; 1 John 2:2).

On the sixth day, after making a covering for sin, God created man.

> God said, Let us make man in our image, after our likeness: and let them have dominion over the fish of the sea, and over the fowl of the air, and over the cattle, and over all the earth, and over every creeping thing that creepeth upon the earth. So God **created** man in his own image, in the image of God **created** he him; male and female **created** he them. (Genesis 1:26–27)

The word *created* is used three times, indicating an absoluteness, no exceptions, not to be doubted or questioned. On the sixth day God created man, in His image and likeness spirit beings, male and female, He created them.

Knowing man would sin, at the end of the sixth day God never saw man as good. And Jesus, saying only what His Father commanded him to say (John 12:49), said that no man is good— only God is good (Luke 18:19).

> God blessed them, and God said unto them, Be fruitful, and multiply, and replenish the earth, and subdue it: and have dominion over the fish of the sea, and over the fowl of the air, and over every living thing that moveth upon the earth. And God

said, Behold, I have given you every herb bearing seed, which is upon the face of all the earth, and every tree, in the which is the fruit of a tree yielding seed; to you it shall be for meat. And to every beast of the earth, and to every fowl of the air, and to every thing that creepeth upon the earth, wherein there is life, I have given every green herb for meat: and it was so. And **God saw every thing that he had made, and behold, it was very good**. And the evening and the morning were the sixth day. (Genesis 1:28–31)

On the second day, when God made the firmament, he never saw the firmament was good. On the sixth day God saw everything He had made — the firmament, the two great lights, and the beast of the earth together were very good. From the things that God made His eternal power and His divine nature for the salvation of mankind can be seen.

THE COVENANT AND THE LAW

The Abrahamic covenant began with God asking Abraham to leave his homeland in ancient Mesopotamia. God promised to bless Abraham with land, and to make his descendants into a great nation through whom God would redeem all people. The first chapter of Matthew's gospel begins with the genealogy from Abraham to Jesus Christ (Matthew 1:1–16).

The command God gave to Adam was intended to bring life, instead it brought death (Romans 7:10). From Adam to Moses sin was in the world, yet because there was no law, no penalty could be paid to satisfy sinning (Romans 5:13). Death reigned from the time of Adam until the time of Moses (Romans 5:14).

The Mosaic law provided a way for the blood of an animal to be a temporary covering over sin (Leviticus 17:11). In addition to the law, the priesthood, the Ark of the Covenant, the tabernacle, and God's Feast Days are all shadows in the Old Testament to Jesus Christ in the New Testament.

"I know the thoughts that I think toward you, saith the Lord, thoughts of peace, and not of evil, to give you an expected end. Then shall ye call upon me, and ye shall go and pray unto me, and I will hearken unto you. And ye shall seek me, and find me, when ye shall search for me with all your heart. And I will be found of you, saith the Lord." (Jeremiah 29:11–14)

JESUS IS OUR SAVIOR

We ourselves also were sometimes foolish, disobedient, deceived, serving divers lusts and pleasures, living in malice an envy, hateful, and hating one another. But after that the kindness and love of God our Saviour toward man appeared, not by works of righteousness which we have done, but according to his mercy he saved us, by the washing of regeneration, and renewing of the Holy Ghost; which he shed on us abundantly through

Jesus Christ our Saviour; that being justified by his grace, we should be made heirs according to the hope of eternal life. (Titus 3:3–7)

JESUS IS OUR GREAT HIGH PRIEST

Seeing then that we have a great high priest, that is passed into the heavens, Jesus the Son of God, let us hold fast our profession. (Hebrews 4:14)

GOD IS EL SHADDAI

But there is a spirit in man: and the inspiration [breath] of the Almighty giveth them understanding. (Job 32:8)

CHAPTER 8

DAY 7 – THE GENERATIONS OF MEN

The original Hebrew writings of the Old Testament did not include the divisions for chapters and the numbering of verses that we have in our Bibles today. They also were not included in the Greek or the Latin translations of those writings. The Masoretic text is the translation of the Greek back into the Hebrew, from which the King James Version of the Bible was translated, that also did not include the divisions for chapters and the numbering of verses. To make Scripture referencing easier chapter divisions were added in the early thirteenth century, but wasn't until the sixteenth century that verses were numbered.

In Genesis, the chapter break divides the seventh day from the first six days. However, the seventh day belongs with the first six days, without it, the story of salvation is lost. This is what Moses wrote:

God saw every thing that he had **made,** and, behold, it was very good. And the evening and the morning were the sixth day. Thus the **heavens** and the earth were finished, and **all the host of them**. And on the seventh day God ended his work which he had **made**; and he rested on the seventh day from all his work which he had **made**. And God blessed the seventh day, and sanctified it: because that in it he had rested from all his work which God **created and made**. (Genesis 1:31–2:3)

When the sixth day ended God saw His work was very good. The heavens (now plural) and the earth were fully restored, it it was finished. Any person placing their faith in God would be *counted* as righteous (Genesis 15:6; Romans 4:13; James 2:23) until salvation would be *received* by God's grace through faith in the blood of Jesus.

At the end of the sixth day all of God's angels, "all the host of them" were organized for war. Satan will rebel against God until the day of the final judgment.

The seventh day is the only day that does not end with "There was evening and there was morning". We are still living in the seventh day, the day of salvation (2 Corinthians 6:2).

If the seventh day was included in the first chapter of Genesis, the second chapter would begin:

These are the **generations of the heavens and of the earth** when they were created, in the day

that the Lord God made the earth and the heavens.
(Genesis 2:4)

When the generations of the heavens and the earth ended the day of salvation began. "The Lord God had not [yet] caused it to rain upon the earth, and there was not a man [suited in flesh] to till ground. But there went up a mist from the earth, and watered the whole face of the ground" (Genesis 2:5–6).

THE GENERATIONS OF MAN

On the sixth day God created man (male and female) in His image and likeness. The first record of the generations of man is found after Adam sinned in Genesis 5:1–32.

> This is the book of **the generations of Adam.**
> In the day that God created man, in the likeness
> of God made he him; male and female created
> he them; and blessed them, and called their name
> Adam, in the day when they were created. (Genesis
> 5:1–2)

The generations from Adam to Noah and his three sons spanned approximately fifteen hundred years. Through Noah God divided the nations of the earth (Genesis 10:32).

The generations from Noah's son Shem to Abram consist of approximately five hundred years (Genesis 11:10–26). Through Abraham God cut a covenant that allowed Him to send His Son to die for all men (Genesis 17:7).

Approximately five hundred years passed from Abraham to Moses. God gave Moses His name as a lasting remembrance (Exodus 3:15; Psalm 45:17). From Moses came God's Feast Days, His law, the tabernacle, and priesthood. Then came the judges, prophets, kings, and the temple, all of which are types and shadows to Jesus Christ.

From Moses to the birth of Jesus Christ was approximately fifteen hundred years, for a total of four thousand years from when Adam sinned to the birth of Jesus Christ.

SALVATION

Salvation "was given us in Christ Jesus before the world began" (2 Timothy 1:9). Hebrews chapter 11 is sometimes referred to as the faith chapter because it lists the names of some of the heroes of faith who were counted as righteous in the Old Testament.

"By faith Abel offered unto God a more excellent sacrifice than Cain, by which he obtained witness that he was righteous" (Hebrews 11:4).

Noah built an ark and became heir of the righteousness that comes by faith (Hebrews 11:7).

Abraham, Sarah, Isaac, Jacob, Moses, Rahab and many other men and women died "not having received the promises, but having seen them afar off, and were persuaded of them, and embraced them, and confessed that they were strangers and pilgrims on the earth." (Hebrews 11:13).

The power of God to save mankind from sin was from before

God created the heaven and the earth, and salvation has always been through faith in Jesus Christ.

GOD'S PROMISES

These are the four promises God gave to Moses when sending him to Egypt. They still apply to anyone who by faith chooses to trust and obey God.

1. I am the Lord, and I will bring you out from under your burdens.
2. I will rid you of bondage.
3. I will redeem you with a stretched-out arm and with great judgments.
4. I will take you to me for a people, and I will be to you a God: and ye shall know that I am the Lord your God. (Exodus 6:6–7)

The Jewish people celebrated these four promises on the Feast of Passover, sharing a meal they called the Seder. During the meal each person drank from four cups of wine, each representing one of God's promises.

1. The first was the cup of sanctification. *Sanctification* means to be separated, to be brought out, to be divided from that which is unholy in order to be made holy to God.
2. The second was the cup of deliverance. *Deliverance* means to be set free, to be rid of that which holds us captive.

3. The third was the cup of redemption. *Redemption* is the act of buying back or taking the punishment for a wrong someone else has committed.

4. The fourth was the cup of restoration. *Restoration* is man being brought back to God. No longer counted as righteous, but made to be the righteousness of God in Christ Jesus (2 Corinthians 5:21).

Before His crucifixion Jesus shared the Seder with His disciples (which we know as the Last Supper). During that meal Jesus drank from only the first three cups of wine. He did not drink from the fourth, the cup of restoration. After drinking from the third cup, Jesus closed the meal, saying:

> I say unto you, I will not drink henceforth of this
> fruit of the vine, until that day when I drink it new
> with you in my Father's kingdom. (Matthew 26:29)

"And when they had sung an hymn, they went out into the mount of Olives." (Matthew 26:30).

Hours later, Mary, the mother of Jesus, her sister (also named Mary), her husband, Cleophas, Mary Magdalene, and the disciple John stood at the foot of the cross when "Jesus knowing that all things were now accomplished, that the scripture might be fulfilled, saith, I thirst" (John 19:28).

Jesus knew that in shedding His blood He had paid the penalty for sin. He thirsted to drink from the fourth cup. He thirsted for all people to be restored to Him.

Now there was set a vessel full of vinegar: and they filled a spunge with vinegar, and put it upon hyssop, and put it to his mouth. (John 19:29)

I wonder if the person who put the sponge on a hyssop branch knew that more than fifteen hundred years earlier, at the first Passover, the Israelites used a hyssop branch to apply the blood of the sacrificial lamb to the door frames of their homes (Exodus 12:22).

After Jesus drank of the vinegar, He said:

It is finished: and he bowed his head, and gave up the ghost. (John 19:30)

In Genesis, at the end of the sixth day God finished His work, and at the end of the sixth day Jesus had paid a debt He did not owe (Romans 5:8).

A rich man named Joseph, who was a disciple of Jesus, asked Pilate for Jesus's body. With the help of Nicodemus, Joseph took the body down from the cross and placed it in a tomb before sunset, when the Sabbath day began (Matthew 27:57–60; Mark 15:42–46, Luke 23:50–54; John 19:38–42).

WHERE WAS JESUS?

Where was Jesus when His body was in the tomb? The disciple Peter says, "Being put to death in the flesh, but quickened by the Spirit: by which also he went and preached unto the spirits in prison" (1 Peter 3:18–19).

In Luke 16:19–31, Jesus told a parable about a beggar named Lazarus, who sat at the gate of a rich man's house begging for the crumbs that fell from the table. When Lazarus died, angels carried his spirit and soul into Abraham's bosom. But when the rich man died, his spirit and soul were buried in hell, where he was tormented.

When the rich man saw Abraham afar off, and Lazarus in his arms, he called out to Father Abraham, asking that Lazarus be allowed to dip the tip of his finger in water and bring it to cool his tongue from the flames.

Abraham reminded the rich man of the good things he had received during his lifetime that he used for evil, and of the huge gulf between them so no one could pass from one side to the other.

The rich man asked Abraham to send Lazarus back to Earth to warn his five brothers so they would not end up in the same place of torment. Abraham answered that if they hadn't listened to Moses and the prophets, they would not be persuaded even if someone rose from the dead.

The bosom of Abraham and the rich man's hell were each a type of prison. The difference is that those in the bosom of Abraham, having put their faith in God, were counted as righteous. Those in hell were the unrighteous, the unbelievers who had rejected the word of God spoken by His prophets.

On the Sabbath day, while the body of Jesus lay in a tomb, Jesus went to the bosom of Abraham. There He preached to those who having been counted at righteous were waiting for the fulfillment of God's promise.

THE FIRST DAY

At sunset the Sabbath ended, while it was still dark, Mary Magdalene went to Jesus's tomb. Finding the stone rolled away she ran to Simon Peter and John saying that someone had taken Jesus's body out of the tomb, and she didn't know where they had lain Him.

The disciples hurried to the tomb and finding it empty, they went home. Mary stood outside the tomb, weeping. Stooping down to look inside the tomb, she saw "two angles in white sitting, the one at the head, and the other at the feet, where the body of Jesus had lain." (John 20:12).

They asked her why she was weeping. She said, "Because they have taken away my Lord, and I know not where they have laid him" (John 20:13). When she said that, "she turned herself back, and saw Jesus standing, and knew not that it was Jesus." (John 20:14). Thinking it was the gardener, Mary asked if He had taken the body. When He called her by name, she recognized He was Jesus. She answered, "Rabboni; which is to say, Master" (John 20:16).

Jesus asked her not to touch Him, saying that He had not yet ascended to His Father. But she was to go tell the others that He had risen.

Matthew wrote, "Graves were opened; and many bodies of the saints which slept arose, and came out of the graves after his [Jesus's] resurrection, and went into the holy city, and appeared unto many" (Matthew 27:52–53).

While hell is still a real place, the bosom of Abraham (or

perhaps what some believe to be purgatory) no longer exists. When Jesus rose from the dead, Abraham, Lazarus, and all those counted as righteous received their salvation and followed Jesus to His Father in heaven.

John wrote that on that "same day at evening, being the first day of the week, when the doors were shut where the disciples were assembled for fear of the Jews, came Jesus and stood in the midst, and saith unto them, Peace be unto you. And when he had so said, he shewed unto them his hands and his side. Then were the disciples glad, when they saw the Lord" (John 20:19–20). Forty days after Jesus rose from the dead, He ascended into heaven (Acts 1:3–11).

JESUS IS THE SON OF MAN

The Son of man must suffer many things, and be rejected of the elders and chief priests and scribes, and be slain, and be raised the third day. (Luke 9:22)

JESUS IS THE LIGHT OF THE WORLD

Then spake Jesus again unto them, saying, I am the light of the world: he that followeth me shall not walk in darkness, but shall have the light of life. (John 8:12)

JESUS IS THE LIVING GOD

When Jesus came into the coasts of Caesarea Philippi, he asked his disciples, saying, Whom do men say that I the Son of man am? And they said, Some say that thou art John the Baptist: some, Elias; and other, Jeremias, or one of the prophets. He saith unto them, **But whom say ye that I am?** And Simon Peter answered and said, Thou are the Christ, the Son of the living God. (Matthew 16:13–16)

CHAPTER 9

TO DAY

Before His ascension, Jesus commanded His followers not to leave Jerusalem, but to stay, and wait for the Father's promise. They would be baptized with the Holy Ghost (Acts 1:4–5). Ten days later, on the day of Pentecost, "there appeared unto them cloven tongues like as of fire, and it sat upon each of them. And they were all filled with the Holy Ghost, and began to speak with other tongues, as the Spirit gave them utterance" (Acts 2:3–4).

God's Holy Spirit gave (and still gives) life to His church, bringing gifts of wisdom, knowledge, faith, healings, the working of miracles, prophecy, discerning of spirits, tongues, and interpretation of tongues (1 Corinthians 12:7–10).

Many were asking what they needed to do to be saved, and Peter said "Repent, and be baptized every one of you in the name of Jesus Christ for the remission of sins, and ye shall receive the gift of the Holy Ghost" (Acts 2:38). In one day the church grew from 120 (Acts 1:15) to about 3,000 people (Acts 2:41). Stephen was one of seven men chosen to oversee their needs.

After Stephen's stoning there came a great persecution against the Christian Church centered in Jerusalem (Acts 8:1; 9:1). Saul was on his was to Damascus with orders from the chief priest to arrest any man or woman who believed Jesus rose from the dead and ascended into heaven. He was to bring them to Jerusalem where they would be slaughtered for their faith (Acts 9:13–14). While on his way, suddenly there was a bright light from heaven that shined all around Saul. Falling to the ground he heard a voice saying to him "Saul, Saul, why persecutest thou me? And he said, Who art thou, Lord? And the Lord said, I am Jesus whom thou persecutest: it is hard for thee to kick against the pricks." (Acts 9:4–5).

Saul had witnessed the stoning of Stephen, and he heard Stephen, just before he died, cry out in a loud voice asking God to forgive the men who killed him (Acts 7:60). His prayer for forgiveness *pricked* Saul's heart. Forgiveness was prodding Saul in the way God had for him to go.

Blinded by the light, Saul was taken into Damascus to the home of Judas who lived on Straight Street (Acts 9:11). Ananias was sent there by God to pray for Saul, and when he did "immediately there fell from his eyes as it had been scales: and he received sight forthwith, and arose, and was baptized" (Acts 9:18).

Years later Saul, whose name was Paul, wrote his second letter to Timothy from his prison cell in Rome. Knowing he would soon be executed for his faith Paul was at peace. "For I am now ready to be offered, and the time of my departure is at hand" (2 Timothy 4:6).

In this, his last letter, Paul reminds us to live our life well "according to the promise of life which is in Christ Jesus" (2 Timothy 1:1). "Who hath saved us, and called us with an holy calling, not according to our works, but according to his own purpose and grace, which was given us in Christ Jesus before the world began" (2 Timothy 1:9).

LIVE LIFE WELL

God's forgiveness and mercy leads us into the life God has planned for us. That life begins with a prick of the heart. Trusting in Jesus, repenting of sin, and inviting Jesus into our life restores our spirit.

The God of all truth is revealed in Scripture ... to anyone who earnestly desires to know Jesus. I pray you receive Jesus into your life, and be baptized in the Holy Spirit. Live your life well, according to the promises of life which are yours in Christ Jesus.